Uncovering G
Book thr

The morn was fine, the day was clear,
The sun auspicious shone;
Th'assembled groups from far and near,
Were met at Gateshead town;
To do a thing not often done
Upon Ascension Day;
The thought elated everyone
Drest up in best array
With colours flying, on they hied,
The people string stood,
To see them plod the water-side
Up to the knees in mud

The Perambulation song written by William Stephenson
who kept a school on Church Walk.

Sandra Brack and Bob Dixon
Gateshead Local History Society

Gateshead Local History Society

The map below shows the actual boundary of Gateshead and
Gateshead Fell in 1850.

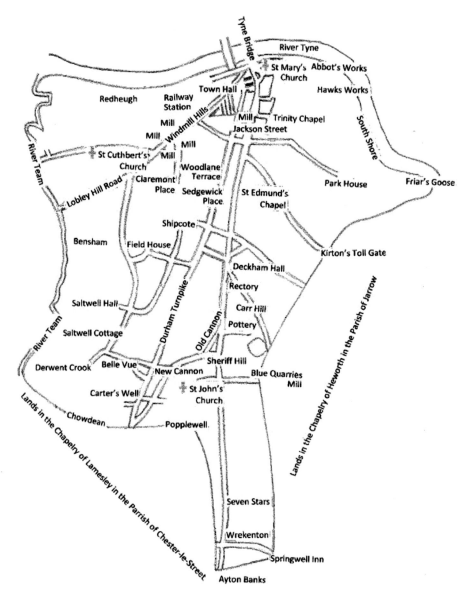

Uncovering Gateshead – Book three
The Perambulation of Gateshead's Boundaries

In this final book of three, the authors take you on their version of the Perambulation of Gateshead's Boundaries. Our walk does not adhere to the actual boundary but is a more practical interpretation of the route due to present day restrictions. It is split into five sections with good transport links throughout Gateshead.

In this context perambulation means walking the confines of your parish in the days when maps were not readily available and was done to ensure the memory of this was passed down through the generations. Young boys struck the boundary stones with a stick hence the term 'Beating of the Bounds'. The Perambulators were accompanied by the clergy who give blessings that the town perimeters would be safe. Any encroachments on these would be torn down.

The Perambulations were discontinued in 1792. The Rector of Gateshead John Collinson revived the Perambulation on Ascension Day, 27 May 1824, as shown in the newspaper cutting below.

Boundaries of Gateshead Parish.

THE PARISHIONERS of GATESHEAD, and all other Persons interested, are requested to meet the Rector, Four-and-Twenty, and Churchwardens, of the said parish, at Gateshead Church, on Thursday the 27th day of May instant, at half-past 8 o'clock, for the purpose of accompanying them in perambulating the boundaries of the parish.

The procession will be at Tyne Bridge at 9 o'clock, from which place it will proceed on the northern boundary to the mouth of the Team. It will then proceed along the western, southern, and eastern boundaries, and conclude with the remaining part of the northern boundary.

By Order,
JAMES CHARLTON, Vestry-Clerk.
Gateshead Vestry, May 10th, 1824.

When they reached Wrekenton 'they partook in bread, cheese and ale', provided by the Church Wardens. After refreshments several of the gentlemen joined in a merry dance upon the green with the 'bonny' Wrekenton lasses.

From Wrekenton they proceeded to Friars Goose and from there to the Tyne Bridge. The walkers then sat down to a dinner at the Black Bull Inn.

This special boundary token was created to commemorate the event in 1849. The last known Perambulation was in 1857.

This historic event was revived in 2011 by Richard Stevenson, Education Officer at St Mary's Heritage Centre, then resumed in 2013 by Simon Green of St Mary's Heritage Centre. Since 2014 the walk has been organised by Gateshead Local History Society.

We hope this book will be enjoyed by everyone whether you are a walker, interested in local history or want to find out more about Gateshead. The walk is approximately 10 to 12 miles (16 to 19 kilometres) and will include some ascent and descent over a variety of surfaces.

Acknowledgements

The authors would like to thank Gateshead Library, Tyne and Wear Archives, Peter Annable, Andrew Clark, Edwin Dodds, Trevor Ermel, Anthea Lang and Jim McParlin.

Also thanks to all those unnamed people who kindly gave us their support.

Bibliography

History of Gateshead – F.W.D. Manders 1974
Ordnance Survey
www.gateshead.gov.uk   www.twsitelines.info
www.englandsnortheast.co.uk

Front cover: St Mary's Heritage Centre, 2018. Boundaries dinner ticket, 1824. Boundary token, 1849.

Back cover: Perambulators, May 2018. Boundary Cottage stone sign.

Our first section covers from St Mary's Heritage Centre to the Kittiwake Tower.

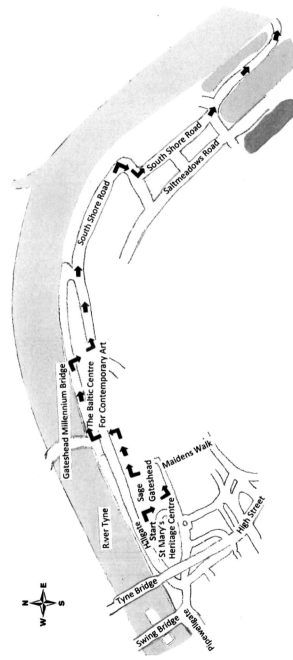

We start our Perambulation at the 12th century mother church of Gateshead now St Mary's Heritage Centre. If you have time, go in and have a look around.

As we leave St Mary's take in the wonderful view of the Tyne Bridge.

We are now in the square where once stood the Rectory of St Mary's built in the 18th century (*shown on next page*). Part of the building was later used as the Brandling Arms, and later a Co-op store in 1861-63. By the 1880s it was a store for the North East Railway, and then as offices for a gas and water company. It was mostly demolished in 1914.

Here now stands The Sage Gateshead, designed by Foster and Partners, a centre for musical education, performance and conferences, which opened in 2004. Preparation for the Sage began in the early 1990s, when the Northern Sinfonia orchestra, with encouragement from Northern Arts, began working on plans for a new concert hall.

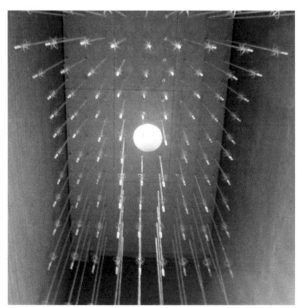

We now walk behind the Sage Gateshead past the street art in the arches to the lifts that take you up to the Sage car park area. Here glance upwards, above you is the magnificent 'Ceiling of stars' designed by Jo Fairfax (2004). The artwork consists of a collection of one hundred and sixteen fibre optic cables of changing coloured light.

From here continue to Maiden's Walk. Observe the old coal drops where coal fell through chutes on to a lower level to be loaded on to ships docked on the south bank of the Tyne. If you

look to the side wall on some of the arches you will see a recessed section, here a man would stand to help the coal along its way. Imagine how dangerous it would be standing there as tons of coal rushed down the chutes, with all the noise and the dust.

Now walk towards the 'Ribbon of Colour' railing designed by Kate Maestri (2004) next to the Sage Gateshead.

Walk past the outdoor theatre area and down the steps on to South Shore Road. Did you notice this strange sign on your way down?

We now cross over to Baltic Square, this area was once a Marble Works. In front of you is the fabulous Gateshead Millennium Bridge which tilts every day at 12 noon between 23 May and early September operated by six hydraulic rams, a fantastic sight.

Now to your right is the Baltic Centre for Contemporary Art which opened in 2002 on the site of the former Baltic Mill built by the Rank Hovis Company to a late 1930s design by architects Gelder and Kitchen. Completed in 1950 and extended in 1957 with the addition of an animal feed mill, it closed in 1981.

At about 11.30pm on Friday 12 July 2002 a friend and I headed to Gateshead Quayside to see the opening of the Baltic Centre for Contemporary Art. We joined the queue along South Shore Road which stretched before us along the footpath, down the steps then weaved back and forth on Baltic Square. At 12.00 midnight came an announcement that The Baltic Centre for Contemporary Art was officially open, this was followed by a large cheer from the crowd. Then searchlights were shone into the sky and waved from side to side. Slowly the queue began to move. We zig zagged back and forth and an hour later we reached the main entrance and were handed two bread buns with 'B-read' on them. We also received a cloth bag containing information on the displays which I still have today. We went to the top of the building in the glass lift and made our way down viewing the displays on each level which included huge gongs and fantastic models of the bridges over the River Tyne. It was a very memorable occasion.

Sandra Brack

In 2012/13 members of Gateshead Local History Society worked on the Young Roots Project with Baltic staff and local young people. Practical workshops developed specific heritage based skills

and research which resulted in a Time Telescope (*shown above*), an interactive learning tool enabling visitors to turn back the clock and imagine life through the years and to see the change of the local landscape.

We now take the path by the river past the Baltic to rejoin South Shore Road. Turn left and follow the road, this area was once Holzapfel's Paint Works. As we follow the road around to the right notice the high stone and brick wall on your left.

Now take the first left still on South Shore Road. It is along this stretch of river front that Isaac Charles Johnson had his Cement Works, shown below in 1850.

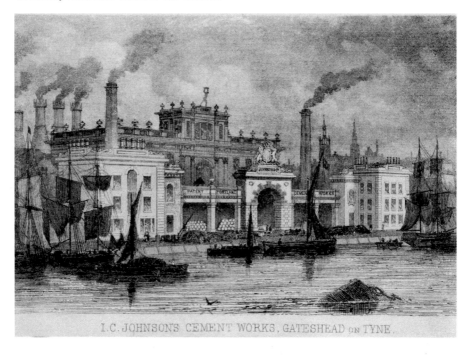

I.C.JOHNSONS CEMENT WORKS, GATESHEAD on TYNE.

Near the end of South Shore Road, on your left you will pass a red brick wall showing weather damage. Now follow the road around to your left to the grass and paved area.

The next section covers South Shore Road to Sunderland Road.

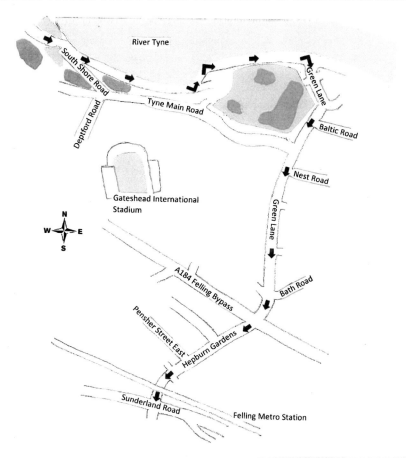

We now take the footpath and turn down to the river's edge. First you will pass the Kittiwake tower built in 2003 as an alternative nesting opportunity to their traditional sites of the Tyne Bridge and the Baltic.

Taking the footpath to your left walk along the path and through the car park, this was the site of Allhusen's Chemical Works.

At the junction our route goes to the left. The road ahead takes you to the Schooner pub which has been known previously as the Ship Inn/Hotel and locally as 'The Bunk' and has an interesting history. A former manager was Billy McParlin who had worked as a pitman and was a very good oarsman. In 1919 he won £100 in the annual Christmas boat sprint from the Redheugh to Swing bridges. He died in the pub and his ghostly presence haunts it to this day.

As we walk along the river's edge we will pass where Gaddy & Lamb, who built wooden ships, had their yard and slipway.

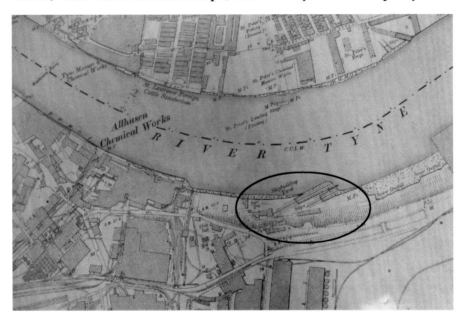

You can see the Gaddy and Lamb Tyne Main Slipway on the 1858 map above.

Not much further along you will see a wooden jetty harking back to the area's former industrial past.

Continue along the riverside path until you come to a high stone wall, behind here once stood a colliery.

Further along past the high wall you will come to Friars Wharf Apartments, follow the road around to the right. This is the site of

Friars Goose Chemical works shown in the sketch below.

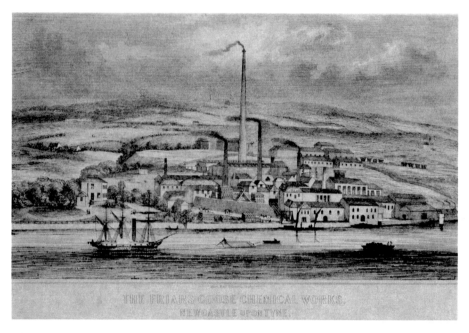

THE FRIARS GOOSE CHEMICAL WORKS, NEWCASTLE UPON TYNE

The Chemical Works opened in 1827 by Anthony Clapham, a soap manufacturer. In 1833 the 263 ft high Clapham Chimney was built, at the time it was the tallest chimney on Tyneside. The chemical works went out of use in 1932 and the recovered land later became East Gateshead Riverside Park in 1966.

We continue past Friars Wharf Apartments where we can see an anchor and plaque commemorating the industrial history of the area.

We now walk up Green Lane towards the Felling Bypass. To your right you can see the remains of Friars Goose Pumping Engine which was erected in the early 1820s. This was used to draw off water from the High Main seam of Tyne Main colliery; there were three sets of pumps, each one 16 inches in diameter.

Below is a sketch of the Pumping Engine in the 1840s.

At the Felling Bypass take the crossing and straight ahead is

HEPBURN GARDENS

named after Thomas Hepburn (1795-1864), founder of the Northumberland and Durham Pitmen's Union.

Walk through the railway arch to Sunderland Road once a turnpike (toll road). This is Felling Gate, to your right stood Kirton's Toll House.

Here there are good transport links if you are doing the walk in stages.

The next section covers Sunderland Road to Windy Nook Road.

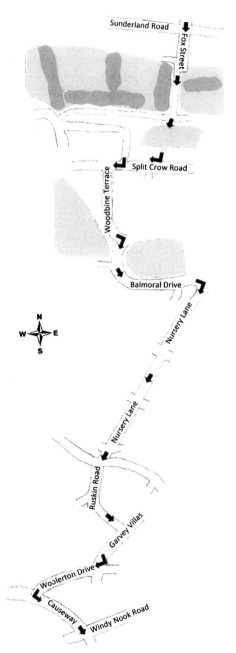

If continuing turn left and take the zebra crossing over Sunderland Road to Fox Street and head up the steep hillside known locally as 'The Bankies'.

My own memory of the Bankies is setting off in the six weeks school holidays with a bottle of water and a jam sandwich, walking up the cemetery walk then up the piggy stairs and along Avon Street on to the Bankies then Split Crow Road and across to the Red Rocks to play soldiers. We were away from 10 in the morning until 4 in the afternoon. Great times.

Peter Annable

At the top of the Bankies turn and take in the view, then continue straight up on to Split Crow Road, cross over and turn right then left into

From here take the narrow footpath at the end of Woodbine Terrace which takes you on to Balmoral Drive. Follow it round,

then turn right on to Nursery Lane and continue to the top. On the corner of Nursery Lane and Carr Hill Road, look up to see this sign on the end house, Greenbourne Village 1711.

Now turn left and walk along Carr Hill Road where you will see this stone street sign, St Albans Crescent 1905.

Retrace your steps, cross over Carr Hill Road and turn left into Ruskin Road and follow it round to its junction with Garvey Villas. We now turn right and walk to the crossroads with

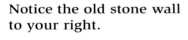

Here we turn right along the narrow footpath passing the old houses (*shown left*).

Notice the old stone wall to your right.

At the end of the street turn left up Causeway. Opposite is the site of Heworth or Snowden's Mill which was built in 1823. The mill was a gristmill which ground the grain into flour and had around thirty employees.

On the corner of Causeway and Windy Nook Road are Hoppers Homes named after Joseph Hopper who was instrumental in providing homes for aged mineworkers.

Now cross over Windy Nook Road to the Greencroft Social Club.

The next section covers Windy Nook Road to Wrekenton.

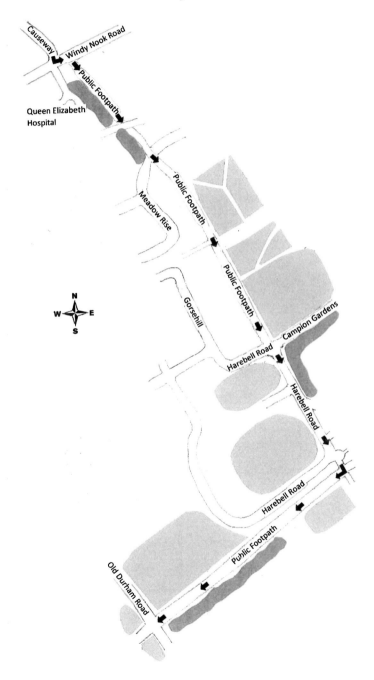

We now take the public
footpath behind the
Greencroft, formerly the
Parliamentary and Urban
District boundary
between Gateshead and
Felling. This area was
famous for its stone
quarries, exporting
grindstones all over the
world. Continue along
this path behind the
Queen Elizabeth Hospital
built on the site of
Sheriff Hill Isolation
Hospital which opened
in 1880.

Cross over Campion
Gardens on to Harebell
Road (*shown bottom
right*). Look to your left
to view one of Europe's
largest environmental
sculptures. This dramatic
landmark named 'Windy
Nook' was designed by
Richard Cole (1986) on a
former colliery slag heap
and covers 5,500 square
metres.

Continue on Harebell
Road until it curves to
the right. Here walk a
little further to the
hedgerow and turn right
on to the Teams Colliery
waggon way, built by
the Liddell family of
Ravensworth Castle in 1670 and extended to Allerdene Colliery
in 1726.

The actual boundary goes further south crossing Springwell Road then a little further turning right on to the old Wreken Dyke Road then right again on to Wrekenton Row and along to Moss Side.

We, however, follow the Teams Colliery waggon way to Old Durham Road.

The photograph below of this area in 1918 shows the Princess Alice and Seven Stars public houses.

We are now on Old Durham Road where there are good transport links if you are doing the walk in stages.

The next section covers Wrekenton to the Aletaster, Durham Road.

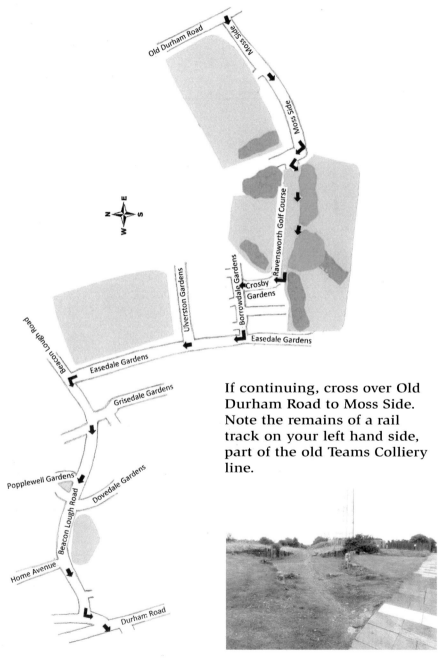

If continuing, cross over Old Durham Road to Moss Side. Note the remains of a rail track on your left hand side, part of the old Teams Colliery line.

As you walk along Moss Side you can see another public footpath off to the left (*shown right*).

Here we have a lovely row of stone cottages built in the early 20th century. Continue along Moss Side turning right into North View until you come to the Public Footpath sign.

Here we turn left entering Ravensworth Golf course, keep to the public footpath crossing diagonally through the trees. (Please show courtesy when crossing as golfers may be playing nearby.)

Below is a postcard of the golf course in 1950 facing north towards Moss Side.

Ravensworth Golf Club was originally founded in 1906 as a nine hole course on land owned by Lord Ravensworth who in 1907 became President. In 1913 the club extended the course to eighteen holes.

At the exit of the golf course you will see this gate which leads you to Crosby Gardens.

Proceed to Borrowdale Gardens turning left then right on to Easedale Gardens and continue to its junction with Beacon Lough Road, passing the former Greenwell/Lyndhurst school grounds originally the site of Greenwell House. Now on Beacon Lough Road turn left, near the bottom you will pass the clinic once the site of Chowdene Head Farm. Then on the corner with Kells Lane is New Biggin Villa where Mr Edward Bainbridge, the Chief Constable of Gateshead, lived in 1954.

Carry on to the corner of Kells Lane and note the row of houses and shops to the left originally called Millrigg Terrace. Here hidden between two shops is an Ordnance Survey flush bench mark 10922.

Now cross Kells Lane at the traffic lights and then over Durham Road towards the Aletaster; a former coaching inn and a convenient stopping point.

Here there are good transport links if you are doing the walk in stages.

The next section covers from the Aletaster to Lobley Hill.

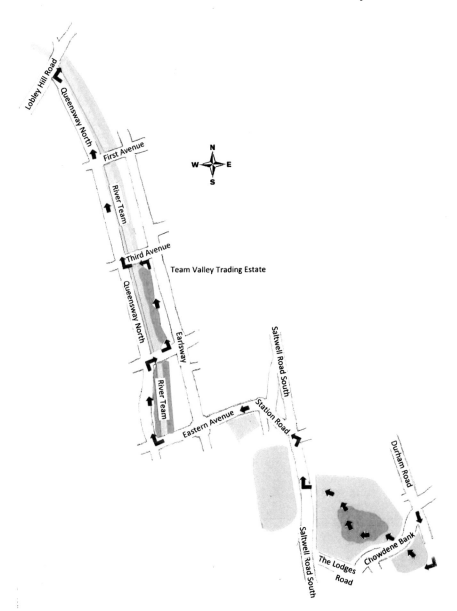

We now cross over Chowdene Bank and walk past Low Fell Library, next you can see the quaint little street Chowdean Terrace.

The two photographs right show the old worn and new street signs.

Glance over the road to the high stone wall of Lyndhurst Bowling Club which opened in 1905. Amongst the club's artefacts is a bell from the cargo ship Maimoa which was launched in 1920 at Palmers, Jarrow. The Maimoa was captured and sunk by the German Navy on 20 November 1940. How the ship's bell ended up at the club is a mystery.

A little way along on your right you will reach two stone houses and a quaint shop front, known as Park View, Durham Road. In 1901 number 1 was the home of the Reverend William Faithful Lumley, the great grandfather of the actress Joanna Lumley.

Continue past the houses and turn right across the grassed area. Compare your view to the photograph below looking over to Glenbrooke from High Row/Chow Dene Grove.

Turn right and walk up Chowdene Bank and cross over to the bus stop. To your right observe the stone sign of Boundary Cottage which marks the boundary with the Chapelry of Lamesley. Now turn left and walk down until you come to a footpath opening on your right. Walk past the steps and take the path parallel with the fence down through the dene. At the corner you can see the faint foundations of Earlswood House, turning right we are now on what was once its carriageway. On the bend take the left path above the grass area until you reach the junction. This is Dodds Dene or Dickie's Dene, named after Dickie Fenwick the local pit owner. Now turn left down on to Saltwell Road South. Alternatively take the path down Chowdene Bank and turn right on to The Lodges Road. Both routes arrive on to Saltwell Road South.

We now turn right and walk toward the zebra crossing. Note the old stone houses on the opposite side of the road. These were originally four sets of semi-detached houses designed by William Lister Newcombe from 1874 and were situated facing over towards the Ravensworth Estate in order to take in the views.

Cross over and turn left down Station Road keeping to the right hand side. We now walk down EASTERN AVENUE

To your left is Breckenbeds Road which is part of the old track that linked The Lodges Road to Derwent Crook Foot Road.

In front of you is the Team Valley Trading Estate, which was the first Government sponsored trading estate in the world, and was formally opened on 22 February 1939 by King George VI.

Before the trading estate was built the site had its own Lido (*shown below*) called the Team Valley Promenade which stretched from the foot of Low Fell Station to Lobley Hill Road and contained a boating lake and paddling pool. It was opened on 14 September 1935 by Alderman W. Hall, chairman of the Unemployment Relief Committee.

Continue down Eastern Avenue, cross over Earlsway to Queensway North and turn right closely following the left hand bank of the River Team. At Fifth Avenue we then cross the river and enter Twenty Pound Close a remnant of ancient woodland alive with bird song and wild flowers.

On reaching Third Avenue we return to the left bank of the river and continue to Lobley Hill Road, where there are good transport links if you are doing the walk in stages.

The next section covers from Lobley Hill Road to Dunston Staithes.

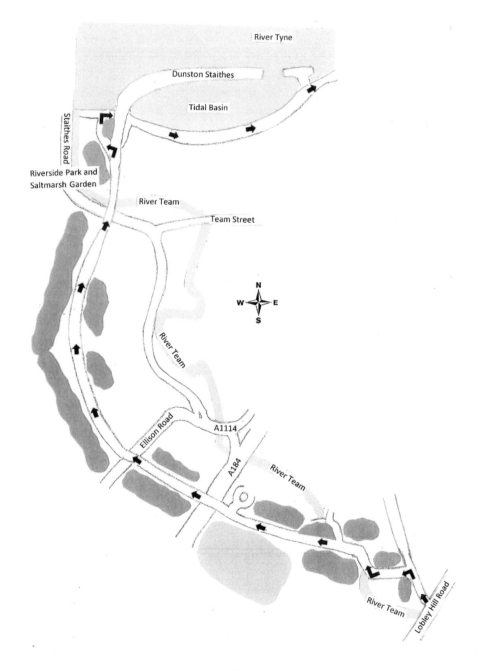

If continuing, cross over Lobley Hill Road and turn right then left, we are now entering the site of Gateshead Garden Festival that took place in 1990. Gateshead's was the fourth of the United Kingdom's five National Garden Festivals. Held between May and October 1990, it lasted 157 days, and received over three million visitors. Attractions included public art displays, a Ferris wheel, dance, music, theatre and sporting events.

The site was created over a two-year period, on 200 acres of derelict land, previously the site of Norwood Cokeworks. After the festival ended, much of the site was replaced by housing.

Take the roadway under the first railway arch, we are now on the Teams Cycleway. Note the decoration on the side of the bridge.

Jennie Moncur was commissioned by British Rail and Gateshead Council to design a paint scheme for the bridges within the Garden Festival site. The project expanded to include twenty two within the Gateshead area.

Walk a little further along and turn left and follow the foot path to a junction.

On your left is the railway arch shown below.

Compare the above photograph to the one below showing the
Caterpillar monorail in 1990.

Now turn right and walk under another railway arch, again note the decorative paint work. During the Garden Festival the area known as Eslington Park was home to the British Rail Exhibition, which was a 36 ft high pyramid made of glass, the Forth Bridge Centenary garden and a wishing well, as well as garden displays, food outlets and play area.

Here you come to an open area where you can see the River Team flowing by, also the remains of a platform from the Garden Festival site.

Take the path to your left and follow it round until you come to a foot bridge over the dual carriageway.

Before you cross the bridge look to your right where you will see the remains of a railway turntable. A locomotive would be driven on to the turntable which would revolve so it could make its return journey.

We now cross over the foot bridge. During the Gateshead Garden Festival this area was known as the Boulevard which had a continental street market theme. Today it gives us our route to Dunston Staithes.

As you cross over observe to your left one of the many decorated railway bridges.

Enjoy the surrounding area as you walk along.

We now cross over Forge Road where we can see another railway bridge to the left. As we continue along we leave the Boulevard and enter Dunston. During the Garden Festival the area housed an Audio Arts 'Radio Garden', a collection of 30 towers each with a short wave receiver and loud speaker. Also an exotic water lily display, festival shopping and events venue.

Carry on along the footpath, crossing over the A1114 and the River Team.

Glance over to the left hand side to view the Riverside Park and Saltmarsh Gardens. Originally created in 1990, using remnants of existing saltmarsh as a reminder of what the area would have looked like. Reopened in 2016 it now contains wild celery, scurvy grass and sea clubrush and is a haven for wildlife.

As you come to the fork in the track you will take the left hand path where you will see an information board about the area.

Follow the path round to the right and you will come to another rail bridge.

Now to your right is the wonderful Grade II listed Dunston Staithes, the largest timber structure in Europe. Built by the North Eastern Railway and opened on Monday 16 October 1893. In 1929, 140,000 tons of coal per week was shipped from the staithes, which closed in 1977.

The staithes were restored and reopened for the Gateshead Garden Festival in 1990. In the early hours of 20 November 2003, a section of the staithes was destroyed by fire. The staithes suffered further fire damage in July 2010 and recently in February 2019. Once the centre of the coal industry, now more associated with leisure and culture.

The photograph below is of the bird hide; why not walk down and see what's about.

We now walk along the riverside, where we have modern houses designed by Wayne Hemingway in 2002.

Compare the view above to the similar view during the Garden Festival in 1990.

Now walk parallel to the Tidal Basin along Bede Courtyard and

At one time this was the site of St Omer's Haugh which historically belonged to the medieval hospital of St Mary, Newcastle who presumably named it after the Bishop of Therouanne who died in 670AD.

Here we come to a jetty with stone blocks where you can sit for a while and admire the view. There is also a café nearby. This area was once the Redheugh Gas Works.

We are now standing on the NER Redheugh branch line as shown in the map below of c. 1856.

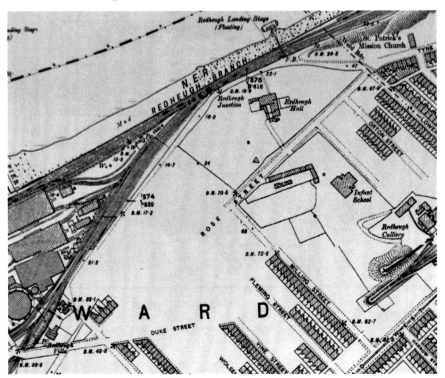

The last section covers Dunston Staithes to St Mary's Heritage
Centre.

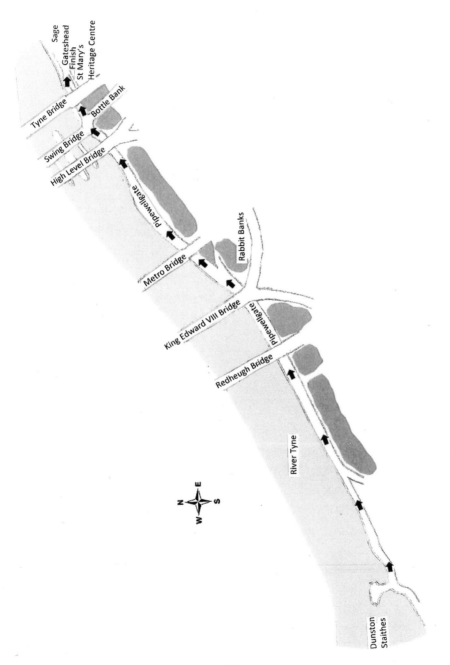

From here walk along
the river's edge passing on
your right a stone bench
engraved 'Riverside'.

As you walk
along take in
the wonderful
view of the
bridges over
the River
Tyne.

Now look
over the
railing, if the
tide is out
you can see
the remains
of a jetty
harking back
to the Tyne's
industrial
past.

A little further
along to your right
and over the road is
the artwork 'Foliate
Forms' by Gilbert
Ward (2010).

Continue along until you see two bollards for tying ships alongside, also notice the interesting old steps leading down to the river. How many feet have passed this way?

If you look up to your right you can see the Toll House for the old Redheugh Bridge. Tolls were removed on Coronation Day 1937.

Here attached to the abutment of the demolished Redheugh Bridge is the art work 'Once Upon a Time' by Richard Deacon (1990), which was inspired by the architecture of the surrounding environment.

We now pass under the third Redheugh Bridge opened in 1983 which has four road lanes and one footpath on the east side. The first bridge at Redheugh was opened in 1871 and the second bridge shown below was built in 1901.

Just past the Redheugh Bridge you will see a stone bench engraved with a fish.

A little further along cross over a wooden bridge.

We now pass under the King Edward VII railway bridge, notice its beautiful red stone abutment. The bridge was opened by King Edward VII on 10 July 1906, and is a Grade II listed structure.

We now pass under the Queen Elizabeth II Bridge which is part of the Tyne and Wear Metro system which was opened by Her Majesty The Queen on 6 November 1981.

Here we are on modern Pipewellgate which stretches from near the Metro Bridge east along to the High Level Bridge. John Whinfield had a foundry in Pipewellgate and reputedly built the first railway engine in Gateshead in May 1805 which moved on a short track within the foundry.

Just past the Metro Bridge to your right you can see the artwork 'Goats' by Sally Matthews (1992) made from recycled materials.

Also, to the left of the goats is the artwork 'Thornbird Railings' by Marcela Livingston (2005), which consist of twenty five panels.

Continue along the riverside footpath until you come to a stone bench engraved 'Gateshead'.

Now glance across the car park where you will see the art work 'Rolling Moon' by Colin Rose (1990).

Follow the path around to your left and glance down.

Notice the heavy metal rings in the cobbles, another reminder of an earlier industrial time.

Carry on along Pipewellgate passing the derelict buildings of Brett's Oils which was established by Richard Freeman Brett in 1877. These buildings stood on the site of Price's Glassworks. This area during the 19th century was very industrial with chemical works, glassworks and manure works.

To your right just before the High Level Bridge, you can see the 'Rise and Fall' artwork which takes the form of a 6m high glass and stainless steel arch, designed by Lulu Quinn (2007).

On your left you will see a white and blue timber building. On this site in 1653 followers of George Fox set up a Quaker meeting room in an old house, this later became the Fountain Inn.

To your right you will see steps leading up to the Hilton Hotel built on the site of an early Roman settlement. At one time there were many steps like these that led from Pipewellgate up to Wellington Street which housed hundreds of people in small tenements built on top of each other, alongside factories and warehouses as shown in the photograph below in 1925.

Now on your left you come to a Grade II listed building, formerly the River Police Station designed by Fenwicke and Watson, architects in 1910. It originally included cells used for holding people illegally entering the Tyne by ship.

From here cross over Bridge Street. To your left is the Swing Bridge designed and paid for by Lord Armstrong and opened in 1876. Note the right hand stone column is only half the width of the other three, why has it been cut in half?

Also note these bumpers on either side of the road to prevent the bridge being damaged by carts.

Glance over to the quayside to see the bars and restaurant which were established for the Great North Exhibition in 2018 and are still there. Take in the view of the Tyne Bridge, shown in the photograph right with the model bridge in front of it. The model located in Saltwell Park having won a silver medal at the Chelsea Flower Show in 2010, was brought to the quayside for the Great North Exhibition in 2018.

Now walk round to your left to Hillgate. On your right is Bottle Bank, the word 'botl' was the Saxon word for house or dwelling.

To your left is 'Blue Beacon' by David Pearl (2004) which marks the pedestrian route along Hillgate. The Beacon is six metres high, with a steel base and translucent acrylic tip and is illuminated at night.

We now walk round to your left to the Tyne Bridge built by Dorman Long of Middlesbrough to the design by Hay and Anderson, and opened on 10 October 1928 by King George V. The bridge houses two plaques. Straight in front of you is a plaque erected by Gateshead and Newcastle Councils to mark the 75th Anniversary of the opening of the Tyne Bridge.

Round to the right is a blue plaque recording the Great Fire of Gateshead in 1854.

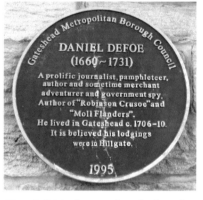

We now cross over Hillgate toward the ramp of Church Walk where you will see a blue plaque to Daniel Defoe, who lodged on Hillgate from around 1706 to 1710. Defoe was a journalist, pamphleteer, author, merchant adventurer, government spy and author of 'Robinson Crusoe' and 'Moll Flanders'.

Walk up Church Walk where you can just see some old stones in the grass banks, possibly the remains of some of the old houses shown in the photograph right.

At the top on St Mary's Square take the narrow footpath alongside the church wall, where you will come to plaques and stones that commemorate the Great Fire of Gateshead in 1854.

Retrace your steps to the entrance of St Mary's Heritage Centre, this is where our Perambulation ends.

We hope you have enjoyed reading/walking the Perambulation of the old Gateshead Boundaries.

Also available

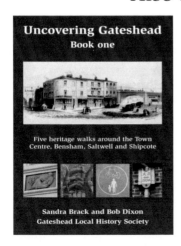

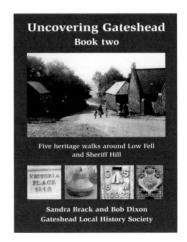